See It
Believe It
Live It

See It
Believe It
Live It

Techniques to Improve Mind Power, Get Inspired, and Achieve Your Goals

MARYAM NASR SARDARI

iUniverse, Inc.
Bloomington

See It, Believe It, Live It
Techniques to Improve Mind Power,
Get Inspired, and Achieve Your Goals

iUniverse books may be ordered through booksellers or by contacting:

iUniverse
1663 Liberty Drive
Bloomington, IN 47403
www.iuniverse.com
1-800-Authors (1-800-288-4677)

ISBN: 978-1-4620-0300-6 (sc)
ISBN: 978-1-4620-0301-3 (ebook)

Printed in the United States of America

iUniverse rev. date: 3/18/2011

To my husband, my best friend, my soul mate.

To my angel, my daughter, my Sophie.

To the most amazing parents—mine.

If you're looking for a "pick me up" book that will give you more courage and strength to get through the day, then *Believe It, See It, Live It* is for you! Maryam Nasr Sardari marries inspirational quotes with true stories and personal insight for a fast and interesting read. I especially enjoyed the "success by accident" stories of Mary Wollstonecraft Shelley and her work *Frankenstein* and the author's own stories of inspiration about her family and her craft and artistry of jewelry-making. I highly recommend reading Maryam Nasr Sardari's *Believe It, See It, Live It*.

—Donna Kozik, WriteWithDonna.com

Acknowledgments

I would like to thank my mentor and colleague, Roger Drew, MS, MFT, LPC, for his continuous support and guidance.

Betsy Knight, MA, ATR-BC, the best supervisor, boss, and mentor. She believed in me when I did not.

Kaveh Sardari, my incredibly talented and supportive husband, without whose smile the sun would stay behind the clouds.

My amazing parents, who always cheer me on.

My supportive brother, whose wisdom I value.

My friends who read everything I write and still remain my friends in spite of it all.

My niece, Sara, who read my first draft and offered valuable feedback. I hope I've done you proud.

Contents

About the Author

Maryam Nasr Sardari, MA, ATR, is a registered art therapist. She has worked with diverse populations both individually and in numerous group settings, including St. Elizabeth's Hospital, residential facilities for emotionally distressed adolescents, alternative schools, and the National Institutes of Health (NIH). Each of these settings demanded her skills in proper interaction with her clients, diagnostic ability to work as a member of a treatment team, and ability to demonstrate different creative techniques in her groups' artistic undertakings. She was also the resident art therapist at Woodson High School in Fairfax, Virginia, where she worked both as an art educator and an art therapist.

Maryam has had training in NLP (Neuro-Linguistic Programming), a technique she has a very strong connection with and has found useful in both her professional and personal life. She is also currently training in ITP (Integrative Transformative Practice) and Bio-feedback. Some techniques from NLP have been mentioned in this book.

Unforeseen changes in budget management and economic turmoil led to early termination of her employment contract from NIH in May 2004, her last place of work. Never having been in such a predicament, Maryam felt quite unnerved and unsure about her future at first. She felt somewhat resentful and upset for having been put in that position until she began seeing her situation in a much more positive light. It became more of an opportunity.

Years of having provided a creative holding environment for patients and clients for their artistic expression had also offered an outlet to Maryam. Many times, at the request of her patients, she would engage in the creative activity along with them. It was in that spirit that she decided to start a business with a lot of encouragement from friends and family. In April of 2006, she and a friend started a company designing jewelry, which is still thriving today.

This venue has been the perfect holding environment. The colors of the gems, the tactile feel of the materials, and the joy of manipulating them to create a design all have contributed to her self-expression. The process of making the jewelry has been even more valuable, for it is Maryam's belief that it is in the process that one learns and grows. The therapeutic aspect of creativity is also invaluable. It is beneficial on so many levels, including an altered state, relaxation, inspiration, joy, learning, and catharsis, to mention a few.

Maryam's creative endeavors include writing, which is an interest she has cherished since childhood. She has a blog: http://www.mydanglingparticiple.com

Introduction

Have you ever been frustrated and overwhelmed by your daily life? What about the pace of life? Everything seems to be moving faster and faster, and it seems as though the harder one tries to catch up, the farther behind one falls. We are surrounded by images and messages telling us what we will be missing if we do not go with the flow. In other words, keeping up with the Joneses seems to be the motto of the day—acquiring more stuff, buying more things. Do we really need all that?

What about our children and the messages they are receiving? Are we setting a good example? Or are we teaching them to be just like what they read in magazines or see on television? Do we teach them about creativity? To realize their potential and be their best and follow their dreams? Their dreams, not ours? Do we tell them to smell the roses along the way and dip their feet in the stream and rest a while?

Talking to our children is only one side of this ever-delicate balance, however. It gives us one thing to contemplate: do we do any of these ourselves? Live by example– isn't this how the saying goes?

Are you happy and content with your life? Do you wish you could have time to pursue your dream? Do you know what your dream is? Do you wish things would slow down so you could have a minute to think? To wind down so you could get your energy back up again? Not be so caught up in the rat race? What would you do if you had the time? What does your dream look like?

In these difficult economic times, it is unseemly not to be concerned about what lies ahead and the prospect of one's children. After all, they are the future, and we must leave them a worthwhile legacy. Why not let them see how motivated and inspired we can be as we pursue our own dreams? They need to see our confidence in our own abilities to achieve our hearts' desires and shape our own futures. This is the best time to demonstrate that hope can be found in the darkest of places, if only one is willing and determine to follow one's path and reach one's goal.

If you agree with this philosophy, then this book is for you. This book is intended to provide motivation and offer useful techniques for concentration to bring about a change in one's state through the use of inspirational and humorous quotes. It will further assert that by changing one's expectations and attitudes, one can change one's outcome.

There are numerous "self-help" books articulating how and what we can do to be more effective in our own lives; however, this book is not meant to be a clinical or academic approach to the fulfillment of one's goals. It is an attempt to further provide insight into achievement through personal stories and other examples. Having been interested in area of self-help and anything motivational and inspirational for many years, I have tried to put together a combination of what I would have liked to have seen in one place. I have drawn from the wisdom of those whom I found effective and inspirational, as well as some personal experiences.

There are also techniques and suggestions about creativity and other outlets as a way to express oneself—to give way to passion and be grateful. The inspirational stories will supply the sideline encouragement.

To see your desired outcome, you must believe it and live it. This book intends to help you do just that—to help you clearly envision your goal and show you different ways to reach it.

So, let us begin this journey together in the direction of our dreams.

I dwell in Possibility—

A fairer House than Prose—

More numerous of Windows—

Superior- for Doors—

Of Chambers as the Cedars—

Impregnable of Eye—

And for an Everlasting Roof—

The Gambrels of the Sky—

Of visitors—the fairest—

For Occupation—This—

The spreading wide my narrow Hands—

To gather Paradise—

Emily Dickinson (#657 I Dwell in Possibility)

Courage/Belief

Most of our obstacles would melt away if, instead of cowering before them, we make up our minds to walk boldly through them! (Orison Marden, www. brainyquote.com)

You gain strength, courage and confidence by which you really stop to look fear in the face. You are able to say to yourself, "I lived through this horror. I can take the next thing that comes along." You must do the thing you think you cannot do. (Eleanor Roosevelt, Activist. www.about.com)

When you consider these quotes for a moment, it becomes apparent that it is mostly our fear that stops us from following our dreams. Perhaps it is the fear of the unknown or the fear of failure. Where to begin? What to do? How many of you have put off starting something you really wanted because you were afraid that it would not succeed?

For many of us, the unknown tends to be frightening, because we do not know what the outcome will be. It is true. The unknown can be very scary. But there is a risk in every venture. Sometimes even things we know can yield different results than what we expected. But without any risk, there is also no learning. There is also the idea of being "comfortable" and "accustomed" to being a certain way and doing a certain thing. Getting out of that "comfort zone" can be disconcerting and unnerving.

When I decided to turn my interest in jewelry making and design into a business, I was terrified for several reasons. One was the fact that I had never run a business, so not only was the outcome unknown but also the path. I had no idea where to begin. The other reason I was terrified was the possibility of failure. What if my venture doesn't succeed? On a more personal level, there was the uncertainty of putting a price on my own creation. How would I be able to determine the value of each piece? Would people understand what the pieces meant to me? I found the task very difficult indeed.

As an art therapist, I always encouraged my clients to take possession of their artwork and own it because they had a tendency to want to discard their artwork or give it away mostly due to low self-esteem and feelings of self-rejection. By encouraging them to keep their artwork, I was trying to instill in them the idea of self-worth. Therefore, it was quite difficult for me to part with something I had put so much energy and time into. However, when I realized that I really enjoyed the process of creation—the creativity itself—and my pieces and were the manifestation of that process, I was more easily able to separate myself from the pieces and found the courage to try the new venture.

One of my favorite authors of all time is J. K. Rowling, the creator of the megasuccessful phenomenon the Harry Potter series. Many of you are probably familiar with her story. It has a great lesson for all of us.

Rowling always knew she wanted to be a writer. She had always seen herself as one in her mind's eye. However, the road to success had several bumps and detours. At a young age, she found herself a single parent trying to make ends meet. She had a long daily commute to work on the train. This is where the idea of Harry Potter first came to her, and she decided to bring the characters to life as a way to pass the time on her commute. Before she knew it, she had the draft of the first book in the series.

Publishers were not as kind and refused her manuscript, but she was determined and kept trying. At last, one publisher agreed to print a small number of copies but suggested that she should write adult stories in the future for better sales.

Well, we all know what happened next. Rarely has there been an author who has been more successful and a story more popular. She and all of her quirky, fantastic characters are household names. The word *muggle* was entered into the Oxford Dictionary (2003). She has created an interest in reading for kids. Even adults enjoy the stories, and through her stories, Rowling has been able to teach many valuable lessons, such as loyalty, courage, perseverance, and friendship.

If she had continued with her less-than-satisfactory job and not pursued her writing—her dream—no one would have enjoyed the magical world she has so masterfully created. If she did not have the courage and belief in her own abilities, she would not have created that opportunity to get the book published, albeit only a few copies at first. She overcame her fear and stepped forward into the unknown. What an immense loss indeed it would have been if she had given up. Thankfully, it was her perseverance and her courage to dream that made it all possible, and I, for one, am eternally grateful for that.

Dare to walk fearlessly into the unknown.

Dare to dream.

> Take control of your destiny. Believe in yourself. Ignore those who try to discourage you. Avoid negative sources, people, places, things and habits. Don't give up and don't give in. (Wanda Carter, writer)

We see courage displayed daily—on the news and sometimes a little closer to home. We hear stories about ordinary people accomplishing seemingly extraordinary goals because they believed they could. It really is this simple; the path to getting there may be unpaved, but the belief is simple. It just needs to be strong and heartfelt. I'm sure you've all had moments when you "just knew" something you expected was going to happen. Of course, I did not mention whether the something unexpected was positive or negative but only that you "knew." That strong sense of "knowing" is nothing but your belief. Although you weren't aware of it, it was you who made it happen.

We've all read about Gandhi—a frail, small man who for all intents and purposes single handedly threw the British out of India and took back his country. His determination ignited a flame that united his country in this effort, all because he strongly believed in his goal. His vision was clear and his path chosen. His belief and courage emboldened others to do the same and put aside their fear. One person can, in fact, make a difference.

He dared to dream.

In addition to facing our fears and faith in our own abilities, it is also important to remember that mistakes will be made. They are part of the journey, and learning takes place through them.

> I've missed about nine thousand shots in my career. I've lost almost three hundred games. Twenty-six times I've been trusted to take the game-winning Shot … and missed. I have failed over and over and over in my life. And that is why I succeed. (Michael Jordan, arguably the best basketball player of all time)

When it comes to excuses, all at once the world seems to be full of inventors. Do not spend half of your life explaining what you would like to do only to spend the other half making excuses why you did not. People only make justifications so others think they have done what in truth they have not. Mistakes have hidden powers to help us, but they stop being effective teachers when we place blame on others. When you make excuses, you give up the power to make a change and improve.

Here is an exercise to help you start envisioning your dream. It is a technique sometimes used as a directive in therapy groups. It is important to mention that the wording has been altered for the purposes of this book.

Close your eyes. Picture yourself entering the lobby of a theatre. You have a ticket. You go inside the theatre, and the usher shows you to your seat. The lights dim, and the curtain goes up. The play begins, and you realize it is about your life. Imagine what the play is like. Who is playing you? Is the story accurate? Is there an ending? Do you agree with the ending? Now, picture yourself entering the theatre again, but this time you are the main character. You're a participant instead of an audience member. How would you alter the scenario? Would you make any changes at all? What about the ending? Picture yourself with your desired finale. Imagine how it feels. See it as clearly as you can. Believe it as if it were reality.

Once you have opened your eyes, you may want to write down or represent the feelings associated with this fantasy artistically. Draw it, sketch it, write it, or color it. Any way that seems most meaningful to you will be sufficient. When you're done, put it somewhere visible. It should be where you can see it easily, perhaps a workspace or the bedside night stand or the refrigerator door. Refer to it as often as you can and recall the feelings associated with it. This repetition will soon link your feelings and vision together automatically. This process is referred to as anchoring. This is a neuro-linguistic programming technique (NLP), which is used to evoke specific feelings on demand.

The more you visit your internal theater, the more specific will be the script and, consequently, the clearer and more lucid the desired ending.

> Nothing contributes so much to tranquilizing the mind as a steady purpose—a point on which the soul may fix its intellectual eye. (Mary Wollstonecraft Shelley)

In 1816, Mary Shelley, her husband, and her stepsister spent the summer near Geneva, Switzerland, at Lord Byron's house (they were good friends). Among the guests there were some of the best known writers of the time. The weather proved to be somewhat stormy and unpleasant for several days, so the whole party decided to have a competition of writing the scariest story. Mary Shelley's story won the competition hands down. We've all heard about it, seen the movie, and even read the book: Frankenstein.

She won because she set out to win. She had a belief in herself and her talent and the courage to try. These were times when women were not considered to be as academic as men, and the ones who found literary or other success often had masculine *nom de plume*. Here was a great opportunity for her to showcase her talent. What better audience and critiques could she ask for? Her story did not only captivate her audience at that time; it has become one of the best-liked stories of all time.

Believing in yourself and what you can do is an absolute necessity to achieving your goal. There will always be naysayers. It is a thousand times easier to criticize than to create. Always remember that being kicked from behind that puts you in front. A Yiddish proverb says, "A critic is the girl who can't dance so she says the band can't play." Close your ears to criticism, because you and only you know how determined you are and how to get to your goal.

> To fear is one thing. To let fear grab you by the tail and swing you around is another. (Katherine Paterson, writer)

Visualization can be a powerful antidote to those pestering voices of self-doubt. These spiritual practices can overpower a lack of confidence and cement a vision of expanded possibilities. Visualizing what you want on a daily basis prepares you to manifest it.

Along with visualizing, you also have to connect with your inner power. This speaks to the power of projection. It is remembering the old axiom "fake it until you make it," which you can employ to help you get through the next hurdle. In other words, if you feel afraid of the unknown, pretend that you are not fearful and that you have already reached your destination successfully. This can also be considered in another way, and that is to work from the end. Working from the end is acting as though you are already living the life you are striving to reach. I do not mean, for example, to spend all your money and deplete all your savings if your goal is to become wealthy. Living from the end is the change you make while considering your goal.

> All I ask is this: Do something. Try something, speaking out, showing up, writing a letter, a check, a strongly worded e-mail. Pick a cause—there are a few unworthy ones. And nudge yourself past the brink of tacit support to action. Once a month, once a year, or just once. (Joss Whedon, Screenwriter, Executive Producer, Director, Composer, and Actor)

It is usually the first step that is the most difficult. Most things seem difficult until they are not, and they are not because someone decided to take a step, a risk, and do it. The physical path may be difficult to travel, but if you believe it is possible to undertake, then it shall be so. You must believe in the outcome and take a leap of faith. More often than not, you will be pleased you did.

Courage depends heavily on fate. If you do not believe in what you want to accomplish and your own abilities, the task will seem next to impossible to achieve. On the other hand, the reverse holds true as well. If it were not for this, man would have never walked on the moon, visited the depths of the oceans, or climbed the highest mountains, and scientists wouldn't have made such incredible discoveries.

Believing in yourself and your outcome—in other words, having faith in what you can do—relies on having a clear vision of your goal. You must see it. See it as clearly as you can. Define it. Be very specific if you can. The clearer the image, the easier it is to see what needs to be done first.

The next visualization exercise is a great way to practice what your goal actually looks like. It helps clarify the image in your mind.

You are sitting in a room on a small carpet. Suddenly, you notice that the carpet is moving. It rises up and up, drifts toward the window, and goes out into the open. You are flying, passing birds and clouds and beautiful scenery. You begin to notice that it is you who is controlling the carpet. Whatever you think, the carpet does. You decide to land. You are going to the land of your dreams, the ultimate destination. The pursuit of your holy grail will come to an end where you land. Slowly, the carpet descends. Finally, it lands. What do you see? What do you feel? Picture it as if you are actually there. Be as clear in your vision and you can.

It is generally helpful to represent your vision artistically. The medium is what you choose. You can write about it, making sure all the details are included, or you can draw it, create a collage, make use of colors or shapes with any medium. Once you feel that your representation is done, display it where you know you will see it every day. This visualization will get easier, and the images will appear clearer as you repeat this process.

The following guided imagery is very useful in confronting angst, worry, and feelings of trepidation. The more you practice these exercises, the more proficient you will be in focusing on your desired outcome.

Close your eyes. Picture yourself taking the walk. You're looking around you, taking in the surroundings. Suddenly, a fog comes down, and you cannot see anything. How do you feel? What do you do? Now the fog lifts as abruptly as it came. What do you see? How do you feel?

This exercise can be applied to a variety of situations. It is a great way to practice taking charge of your own inner obstacles and "fogs." Repetition on a regular basis is highly recommended.

> You can have anything you want—if you want it badly enough. you can be anything you want to be, have anything you desire, accomplish—if you will hold to that desire with dinginess of purpose. (Robert Collier)

It seems as though I am always telling my daughter this very thing. If you want something, really want something, you will find a way to attain it. You will take the necessary steps, despite the fear and uncertainty you may feel, and move forward. It may take a little longer than you like—since children seem to have a different time expectation than adults—but you can get there. Just keep your goal in mind and go for it. My daughter is only nine years old now, but she is beginning to understand this concept.

In second grade, my daughter Sophie struggled with basic math concepts. She felt ill at ease whenever she had homework and realized math was not her forte. As a result, her self-confidence was low, and she was beginning to dislike the subject. One day she asked me if the concept of "you can do anything you want if you want it badly enough" applied to math. I responded with a resounding yes, and she decided to do extra work with a little guidance and encouragement from my husband and me. The following Summer I signed her up at an after school center to get the right instructions, and she made the commitment to work hard. During that school year, she was put in an advanced class and was recommended to a gifted program.

Sophie got to experience the power of mind over matter first-hand. The fact that you can control your own thoughts and will them in a positive or negative direction can be helpful in feeling courageous in moving toward your desired goals. It is about reprogramming your mind to move in a positive direction in the face of disappointments because there is something you really want. You can use your passion and work hard toward realizing your dreams.

The following exercise is an art therapy technique that can be used in many different ways and for many different reasons. It is used as a way to bring some order to chaos or any other feelings you may need/want to explore. I mention it in this chapter because there are times when a sense of chaos and confusion can overpower you and make you feel fearful, discouraged, and powerless.

The word *mandala* refers to a circle. Circle (in Jungian psychology/psychoanalysis) is a primitive mental image inherited from the earliest human ancestors and is supposed to be present in the collective unconscious.

Life can be chaotic at times and cause you to long for balance in your life. The following activity is designed to give you the space so often needed to reflect and search for balance and self-knowledge. Working within a mandala that represents your universe gives you a healthy point for your self-exploration.

The objective of this exercise is to create a special circle that helps you to bring a sense of balance and unity to your life. You will need a pen or pencil; paper or cardboard; a plate or a piece of string and drawing pin; scissors; oil pastels, felt-tipped pens, or paint and paintbrushes.

First, think about and write down the central aspects of your life. Suggestions include hopes, ambitions, fears, and dreams, but there are countless other options.

Next, list some specific examples under each category. Try to balance the size of various life categories so they match how you are feeling at the time. If your fears section has six ideas in it and your hopes section only has four, increase the latter if you are feeling positive.

Now draw a circle as small or large as you wish on your paper or cardboard base. Either draw around a plate or attach a piece of string to your pencil and the end of the string to the center of your paper with a drawing pin. Keeping the string tight, draw your circle with the pencil. Once you have finished, cut out the circle.

Using a felt-tipped pen, oil pastel, or paint, divide your circle into the life categories you have thought about. It is up to you how to do this. Now illustrate each section to reflect how you feel about it and the elements within it. You do not have to adhere to the sections created if you don't feel like it.

Look at your finished work, ask yourself questions about it, and record your feelings on a piece of paper or in a notebook. You might even like to hang it up and use it for further observation (greatly recommended). You can do as many mandalas as you wish.

As you reflect on your piece, consider the following: Did you have more thoughts about some areas than others? Which and why? Were the same areas the easiest to illustrate? Why did you choose the categories you did? Did the process help bring some understanding into your views about yourself? Do you like your finished mandala?

As mentioned before, this technique can be modified to be used in other areas of planning and contemplation. There is no right or wrong way of doing it. It is merely a way that one can create a state change (to be discussed more in upcoming chapters) and be able to project one's feelings onto a physical object.

> Most obstacles would melt away if, instead of cowering before them, we make up our minds to walk boldly through them! (Orison Marden)

Have you ever done something you were avoiding out of fear only to discover that it wasn't that difficult or unpleasant after all?

I've had my share of procrastinations for various reasons, but every time I finally do the work, I realize that what I had imagined was by far worse than reality. To share a personal example, I had been thinking about starting a blog for several months but always hesitated, no doubt due to my own fear and discomfort of being judged. Finally, I decided not to procrastinate anymore, and I conquered my fear. To my delight, I realized that I had blown the magnitude of this task out of proportion. This is true for most things in life. As enticing as our dream and ultimate goal may be, we imagine reaching it to be far worse and grueling than it is.

Do not let fear stop you from achieving your goal.

> If you can put fear aside, you're unstoppable. (Janet Hagerberg, writer and activist)

> And the trouble is, if you don't risk anything, you risk even more. (Erica Jong, writer)

Imagination/Creativity

Creativity is a state of high energy where mental sparks are flying, and the unlikely seems within reach. It is a state that feels infinite, because life is infinite, and creativity makes us feel alive. Even the smallest of the sparks can have a transformative effect within us; as they "tickle" our senses, our emotions are aroused, and our minds open up.

> If you have any talent, use it in every which way possible. Don't hoard it. Don't dole it out like a miser. Spend it lavishly like a millionaire intent on going broke. (Brendan Francis, poet, short story writer, novelist, and playwright)

I love this quote. It really resonates with me. It is like a green light giving me permission to just be creative and do anything I wish that requires me to be imaginative. What could be better than that? It does not matter what the medium is. Everyone has a level of creativity, and it is in that process that one can call on the energy of the universe to work in his/her favor.

The more involved you are in the process of creativity, the more creative you become. Ideas rush in, and the right juices flow. I find that every time I'm designing a piece of jewelry I get many new design ideas. At times, there are so many that I feel overwhelmed. I feel that if I do not make these pieces fast enough, I may forget all the ideas that are coming to me. Sometimes I sketch them, and at other times, I write detailed descriptions of colors and materials. On occasion, I make two or three pieces simultaneously.

> If I create from the heart, nearly everything works; if from the head, almost nothing. (Marc Chagall, 1887–1985, Russian painter)

Creativity is also a great outlet. I find that it is necessary to have an outlet of some sort when you need to de-stress. It provides a change of state. The mind switches gears, if you will, and when you go back to your task, you feel refreshed. It could be as simple as writing a few words backward or holding them up to a mirror and trying to trace them. It puts the mind in a completely different state and distracts it from the pressure of the previous task. It is a welcome distraction. Try something like this and see how you feel.

Having said that, in order to access your creativity, you must first acknowledge and capture your inspirations. They are like cherished little seedlings in need of nurturance. Creative inspirations attract like a magnet. They lure, charm, tempt, and captivate our attention. Whether it is an idea, an impulse, a thought, an intuition, or a feeling, an inspiration can be a strong stimulus to draw us into our creative selves.

> If you have a passion for something, it has an energy to it. (June Levinston, ceramist)

Here is a great exercise that is often used by art therapists. It is called the scribble technique. This method is a great way to wake the imagination and bring out creativity. It is also a great distraction from a labor-intensive project.

Take a piece of paper (preferably no smaller than 8½" x 11"). Draw a random wavy line all the way across the page. Now examine the line for a few minutes and then add what comes to your mind; it can be anywhere—above, below, or to the line. You may also do all three. Once you are done, look at the whole picture. Through this image, you will not only have expressed yourself but also distracted yourself. Now you can resume your previous task feeling refreshed.

> It's not what you look at that matters, it's what you see. (Henry David Thoreau)

This is another important fact to remember. A crucial part of reaching your goal is to be able to see it—really see it. This is why we all have imagination. It's the greatest tool in helping us visualize our goals. The better the visualization, the easier it is to see one's path.

> Imagination is the highest kite we can fly. (Lauren Bacall, actress)

In addition to visualization, it is also helpful to think about what it is we are willing to give up in order to reach our goal. After all, there are always some sacrifices that must be made in the road to success. Knowing what they may be can help us better assess our willingness to undertake this journey.

Try the following visualization. Close your eyes. You are walking along a street in a town. You come to a side street. You've never been on this side street before, so you decide to turn and walk down the side street. Once you begin walking, you notice a shop. You look at the window display and realize that there are a number of unusual objects in there—objects that seem to be from a different time. You decide to walk in. The shopkeeper greets you and invites you to look around. You are awestruck by the objects you see in the store. The shop items seem to have a magical feel to them. You notice a particular item. The shopkeeper points out that no money exchanges hands there, but in place of the item you want, you must give something of yours. Now imagine: what would you be willing to give in exchange for what you really want?

This exercise is helpful in directing your mind toward your goal, and like all others mentioned in this book, it will be more effective with repetition.

When I began my business, I must admit that my goal was not as clear in my head as it should have been. When a friend suggested becoming partners, I felt relieved, because I thought she might have better ideas. Sure, I knew what I wanted, but it was not very specific, and I could not see it in my mind's eye. The images were numerous and blurry, and I never seemed to be able to focus on any of them. There were different images in my head that were ever changing. My partner became confused as a result of my lack of clear vision. She seemed to be clearer with her vision, but our visions did not seem to be the same. There was no clear plan. I just wanted to be there already, but "there" was nowhere in particular. It is not surprising, therefore, that we had difficulty starting our creative venture.

I believe this was a great learning experience and one that, perhaps, I would not have learned as well any other way. Furthermore, we have both realized the importance of keeping the vision and goal as precise as possible. The trick is to create a momentum and keep that image clear. Keep picturing yourself reaching the goal. Better yet, picture yourself already having reached the goal. Imagine how it would feel.

> We need to remember that we are all created creative and can invent new scenarios as frequently as they are needed. (Maya Angelou, poet and writer)

> Trust that little voice in your head that says "Wouldn't it be interesting if …" and then do it. (Duane Michals, American photographer)

What does your goal look like? How would it look if you actually reached your goal? How would you feel? What would you see? Can you imagine being there? What would it take to get there? Imagine not having any obstacles of any kind in your way. What would you need to do to achieve your goal? Picture a smooth, straight road. What would you find at the end of it?

If you were able to answer any of these questions, then you are on your way to achieving your goal. Being able to clearly see the objective in your mind is a sure way of helping you get there.

> Imagination is everything. It is the preview to life's coming attractions. (Albert Einstein, German theoretical physicist)

> Think left and think right and think low and think high. Oh, the thinks you can think up if only you try! (Dr. Seuss, American writer and cartoonist, *Oh, the Thinks You Can Think!*)

Repression, or not having enough confidence in yourself, is poison to creativity. The longer you repress, the harder it becomes to create. Then you'll start saying things like: other people are creative, not me. It is time to stop watching other people live the life you desire. Creativity is any kind of openness to opportunities. When you use your imagination and creativity, you open up a new channel and allow another part of your brain to exercise its muscles. Chances are, more often than not, they will pleasantly surprise you.

> I think the creative process is not about creating something else; it's about the process itself creating who I am. (Mayumi Oda, artist and writer)

We all have creativity hard wired in our system. Creativity is not just for talented geniuses. It is a tool we can all access and utilize. It does not matter if you've never picked up a pen or cannot draw a straight line; you have a creative self waiting to be realized. It's tapping into it that some find trickier than others. Perhaps the reverse holds true as well. The logical, practical, rational side of the brain can also be somewhat trickier for some than others. The point is, however, that we all possess these abilities. We just need to find a way to tap into it. Creative people dare to believe in their insights and to take risks, even if it means being wrong. You are unique; therefore, your inspirations are unique.

Martha Graham (American dancer choreographer) put it quite eloquently:

> There is a vitality, a life-force, an energy, a quickening that is translated through you into action and because there is only one of you in all of time, this expression is unique. And if you block it, it will never exist through any other medium and be lost. The world will not have it. It is not your business to determine how good it is not how valuable not how it compares with other expressions. It is your business to keep it yours clearly and directly, to keep the channel open. … Whether you choose to take an art class, keep a journal, record your dreams, dance your story or live each day from your own creative source. Above all keep the channel open!

Self-focus is an essential component in doing anything creative. Without it, it would be difficult to give in to your inspirations. Thus, in order to produce creative awareness, your state of mind must be in its optimal state—self-focused. The creative process is a kind of dance between the self and the medium; therefore, the self must feel free in order to move to the beat.

Your creative self is alive. It has always been there and waiting for your invitation to blossom and grow. Acknowledge it and embrace it. Let it burst forth and become stronger. Acknowledging your creativity leads you into a life of self-expression and self-fulfillment.

You may agree with all this but think that it would have been helpful if there were something you could do in order to release some creative energy. Here is a little mental game that I find quite helpful: to live creatively free, do what you know how to do now and act as if you know how to do the rest. It is going back to the "fake it until you make it" idea.

Katherine Hepburn (actress) said in an interview, "Oh, I'm scared all the time! I just act as if I'm not."

In other words, take micromovements. Whenever I feel stuck about what to do next with a creative idea, I think to myself, *What could I do now? What tiny step can I take?* Sometimes it is as simple as looking at my stones (gems), and then suddenly an idea comes to me. Tiny movements can cause great creative change. Anyone who has struggled or still struggles with procrastination can benefit from this exercise as well. At other times, I simply take a turn about the room. I make a cup of tea or do anything to distract myself momentarily. This diversion generally seems to kick start my brain, and new ideas form.

In NLP, this is referred to as state change. This state change provides a momentary distraction in one's mind from the task at hand and helps the brain to switch gears into a different mode. State change can also be achieved through sound. Playing a piece of music or tapping on the table can bring about a state change.

So, put on your acting cap on and act out your script. Be true to the scenario you want to reach in your life. Visit that theater again in your mind and participate in the play. Change the scenes according to your liking as much as you want until it is just perfect. Imagine how it feels.

I find that reading other success stories and stories about successful people's journeys to the top is also very inspiring, which, in turn, seems to fuel my creativity. It is the desire to be fearless and daring like they have been and to follow my own path to success. I sometimes spend numerous hours or even days or weeks completely immersed in a particularly imaginative story I have read several times already and revel in the parts that inspire and move me the most. Images are also a great source of inspiration. My imagination always goes into overdrive when I see colors and designs. In other words, I attain creativity from creativity.

Limitations live only in our minds. But if we use our imaginations, our possibilities become limitless. (Jamie Paolinetti, United States National Road Race Champion)

If my mind can conceive it, and my heart and believe it, I know I can achieve it. (Jesse Jackson)

When I was little, I used to love cloudy days. I didn't enjoy the gloominess and the rain in particular, but I loved it when the sky was full of those white, puffy cumulus clouds. I remember looking at them for hours and seeing all kinds of shapes. I would make up stories based on the shapes I saw. They always involved magic, of course, but that was my inducement. There was always a magical castle and winged people along with fairies and a mean-spirited troll or giant who turned out to be good but just unhappy. I imagined myself jumping on the clouds and landing safely and running toward the magic castle. Then I would see all kinds of fantastic objects. I still very clearly remember the excitement I felt. Those clouds and my imagination would provide me with plenty of entertainment, which often turned into ideas, mostly of the design variety, that I would in turn use on my Barbie.

Ideas and possibilities can be found in the most unexpected places. Ever watched a worm or a group of ants move? Ever noticed the minute details on a leaf? Have you ever looked at any kind of imprint on mud? What about closing your eyes and just listening to the surrounding sounds? If one's mind is open to receiving new ideas and possibilities, then they would unveil themselves.

When I worked as an art therapist with adolescents, one of the directives I would give was to have them close their eyes and scribble on black paper with their non-dominant hands. Then they were to look and see what possible images popped up or which lines they could develop into an image. It was amazing what they would see. A regular scribble with the dominant hand on white paper works as well, but the idea of keeping the eyes closed until the scribble is done is so that no one can plan anything. Only the hands are supposed to be moving, letting the mind feel free. It's what is in your subconscious that is supposed to surface. Brilliant, isn't it? Try it, and you'll amaze yourself.

I think the world really boils down to two types of people—those who see shapes in cloud formations, and those who just see clouds. (Danzae Pace, poet)

Let us each follow our imaginations to the clouds and beyond. Let's jump on those fluffy white clouds and look around. We might be amazed by what we'll find.

Possibility/Opportunity

I read a fabulous little story about a shoe factory that sent two marketing scouts to a region in Africa in order to find out the prospects for expanding the business. One sent a telegram back saying, "SITUATION HOPELESS STOP NO ONE WEARS SHOES" The other triumphantly wrote, "GLORIOUS BUSINESS OPPORTUNITY STOP THEY HAVE NO SHOES" (*The Art of Possibility* by Zander and Zander)

Now, wasn't that just a fantastic story? It illustrates the fact that one has the choice to create opportunities for oneself or feel hopeless. Put in another way, when there is a will, there is a way. To the marketing representative who sees no shoes, all the evidence points to hopelessness. His colleague sees the same condition as opportunity. Each scout comes to his own interpretation. We've all heard the saying, "When life hand you lemons, make lemonade." In fact, all of life comes to us in this form. We each tell a story in the way we interpret the world. Some may argue that it is hardwired in our systems—some people are just glass half full types, and others are glass half empty types. However, I don't believe that. I am a strong believer in people carving out their own ways. With a clear vision one can better recognize potential opportunities and see possibilities. When your goal is clearly defined, the steps to reaching it also become clear.

I think we can all agree that life is dangerous enough to be considered an adventure. One never knows what will happen from one moment to the next. But isn't this uncertainty what makes life worthwhile? If you knew every morning what would happen that day and the day after that and so on, your life would become boring, would it not? Perhaps what makes life extraordinary is the fact that we have the power to conceive and achieve our own dreams. After all, what would be the point of an adventure if we did not have some kind of control over its outcome or choose some of the pleasures that would come out of it or the lessons it offers?

You may ask how we best make use of all this "adventure" has to offer. We do so by taking two little steps. The first step is to understand life. For example, when learning to cook, one must first understand how to operate the stove. The second step is to live the life. Using the same example, once you learn how to operate the stove, you still need to prepare the ingredients and cook the meal.

This also speaks to the creative bit as well. When you are determined to do something, you will find creative ways to get it done. People are always more resourceful and creative than they are willing to give themselves credit for. The key is not to lose sight of the main goal and keep in mind that there is always more than one way to achieve the same result.

Do you remember the scribble exercise I mentioned in the previous chapter? The same concept can apply in order to see/bring about possibilities in different settings or situations. If you approach every problem the same way, you are never going to find a new solution. Instead, if you change your approach, the solution will have to be different as well. The scribble represents the new approach. It represents the difficulty that may be seen ahead. It may look like a twisted and jumbled path at first, but in closer inspection, you may see new pathways to the same destination. If you always take the highway to reach your destination, you'll never see the beauty that the scenic route may offer you.

> The pessimist sees difficulty in every opportunity. The optimist sees the opportunity in every difficulty. (Winston Churchill, British politician)

> If opportunity doesn't knock, build a door. (Milton Berle, American comedian and actor)

Very simply put: create your own opportunities. Don't spend your time regretting the opportunities lost; think about the new possibilities you may have gained. We all learn from past mistakes. At least, that's the way it should be. If we've learned anything, then we've also gained the knowledge of other possibilities.

> Opportunities are never lost; someone will take the ones you miss. (author unknown, www.quotegarden.com)

Many of the circumstances that seem to block us in our daily lives may only appear to do so based on our own assumptions. Fear and negativity can cause paralysis of the mind, which will prevent you from seeking new solutions. If we change these assumptions, extraordinary accomplishments can become a daily experience. (I'll share more about this in the next chapter.)

Meditation and breathing exercises can often unblock that flow of thought and create a state change in which to find new ways of approaching the problem at hand. Sometimes getting up from your chair and walking about the room is enough to bring about this change. Once you are aware of other possibilities, you can accomplish your goal more easily.

> If you do what you've always done, you'll get what you've always gotten.
> (Anthony Robbins, American self-help author and success coach)

Try the following guided imagery: You're at the station. Your train is in. You get on and take a seat. The train leaves. It travels for a long time. You're filled with anticipation regarding your destination (you decide what level of anticipation, positive or negative). Suddenly, the train stops. An announcement asks you to get out. You do. You look around. Where are you? Imagine this new place. Are there other people who had to get off too? You notice the train leaving without you. How do you feel? What will you do? Now imagine yourself being calm and feeling relieved and excited that there is a new possibility. You've been given a chance to start over. Think about what you want. Now imagine what it takes to get it done. How does it feel?

The important thing to remember is that before any *doing* there comes the *thought* behind it. When man decided to fly, he first thought about aviation—the possibility that man could create something that could help him fly. Then came the steps to make it happen. So, first come goals, and then they become reality.

Have you ever heard the saying, "Be careful what you wish for, because you just might get it"? I bet you have. I'm also willing to bet that you believe it to a degree. Am I right? But why and how is that do you think? What strange and mysterious force is at work here that can turn dreams into reality? There is a very good chance that you are not superstitious, so what could this be?

You've likely heard about the power of positive thinking or the new buzzwords "the Law of Attraction" (thanks largely to the undeniable success of the best selling book and DVD *The Secret*). Others have spoken about it before but have called it different things—for example, "the Power of Intention" and so on. They all are talking about the same idea. But have you ever wondered what actually makes the Law of Attraction work? Something does.

The simple answer to this quandary is that our thoughts become things! This is the underlying principle that turns dreams to reality, equips positive thinking, and gives rise to the Law of Attraction. This principle is always true. It is unchanging and reliable like the sunrise—not just sometimes but all the time and not just with positive thoughts but all others.

All that being said, this is good news, because it gives us the control to choose our thoughts and, in turn, our words and actions. But the latter is merely the manifestation of our thoughts. So, the message here is that once a thought is thought, it is as though it has been given its own will and power to begin physically attracting the nearest thing it finds as its match. It is up to us, therefore, to choose our thoughts and choose them wisely. But where should we begin? Choosing your thoughts means that you must be aware of what you think at all times.

We all know that there are times in the day when our minds have wandered off, and we've been unaware of a single thought. It does not matter. Just do what you can. Visualization, like the exercise mentioned earlier, is a very helpful tool in guiding your thoughts. However, do not do more than five minutes at a time, or you'll be daydreaming instead.

Take the time right now to write down at least five downtime actions that you can take in the next twenty-four hours that would help you move toward what you want in the big picture. If you want to be an author, maybe it's writing one chapter. If you want to get healthy, maybe it's a one-mile walk or run. Performing give downtime actions per day for one week will create a massive shift in your readiness for opportunity.

I challenge you to come up with your own visualization exercise and let your thoughts and feelings linger on what you really want. Keep in mind that the clearer the image, the easier it is to envision the possibilities and recognize the opportunities. Go ahead; close your eyes and start visualizing.

The Power of Expectation and Attitude

We're bombarded by messages daily. Some we are conscious of, and some we are not. These messages range anywhere from the products we use or should use to socially accepted behaviors. The underlying meaning is the expectations that are put upon us. Some operate on fear and anxiety, such as governmental propaganda and organized religion, while others are more neutral. The current of messages is always flowing, and the external expectations will always be thrown our way. The important thing to bear in mind is that we, too, have expectations—our own expectations from ourselves and what we'd like to achieve. We all have dreams.

Reprogramming ourselves and our attitudes to perform from a positive framework is essential in turning our dreams into reality. Remember, we have the power to choose to change our thoughts and attitudes. Expecting a positive outcome will result in a positive outcome.

> The greatest discovery of my generation is that human beings can alter their lives by altering their attitudes of mind. (William James, American psychologist and philosopher)

This clever quote just about sums up the power of intention and attitude. We all know it in one way or another. We've all heard about the Law of Attraction (discussed in the previous chapter). It refers to the idea that thoughts can influence change.

> Any facts facing us is not as important as our attitude toward it, for that determines our success or failure. (Norman Vincent Peale, minister and author)

In order to develop a positive attitude, you must first become aware of the true nature of your present attitude. This is not always easily done, but how one reacts to different situations generally reveals a great deal about one's attitudes. The key to succeeding in any endeavor is to approach it with a positive attitude. Attitude affects every aspect of one's life and work.

Success requires more than talent. While both talent and knowledge are crucial, the key that unlocks them both is your state of mind. When you are positive, you will notice that you are instinctively more respectful to others and, therefore, more considerate. If you're at work, you will help others do their jobs more efficiently, because you have pride in your work, and your enthusiasm will show through your attitude. In return, this will be noticed and returned back to you.

This law works both ways. Have you ever started to think about something you did not want, and the more you thought about it, the worse you felt? That is because you were keeping a consistent thought—an unhappy one in this case—therefore, you attracted similar thoughts. As a result, you became increasingly upset and unhappy. Just as you can attract unpleasant feelings and thoughts, the reverse is also true. By thinking positive thoughts, you will also attract more of the same.

This chapter is closely related to the previous one because of the fact that one has the power to bring about possibilities. One can bring about possibilities by having the right attitude and having an expectation that one can accomplish what he or she wishes.

> Your circumstances may be ungenial, but they shall not remain so if you only perceive an ideal and strive to reach it. You cannot travel within and stand still without. Let a person radically alter his thoughts, and he will effect in the material conditions of his life. (James Allen, British philosophical writer)

Whether you think you will succeed or you think you will fail, it is almost certain that you will be proved correct. If you have a well-formed outcome, you can make effective decisions about what you will be willing to do in order to reach that outcome. Without a well-formed outcome, you will simply be reacting to your surroundings. The result of that would render you ineffectual and increasingly frustrated and resentful.

When I was at graduate school for art therapy, we had to do placement internships in order to complete the practical requirement of the program. During the first year, I was placed at St. Elizabeth's hospital in Washington, DC working with an adult population with severe psychiatric disorders. I considered myself very fortunate to have been accepted, since the position was full time, stipend, and very much in demand—not to mention the fact that it offered the best clinical experience.

Once I went through the initial orientation, I was assigned different groups that I began to lead. I was full of energy and ideas, convinced that all of my patients were going to be blown away by my skills and my creative ideas for their groups. Mine were going to be the patients to be successfully treated and discharged never mind what their histories or their diagnoses were. With that mind-set, I ran my groups week after week and discussed any issues during supervision—issues that seemed to be growing with the passing weeks. That was most certainly not what I had envisioned or expected. I was unable to understand the underlying cause of my frustration in seeing next to no change in my patients' behavior. I should further clarify that by change I mean a positive one, an improvement.

By the end of the fifth month, I felt my energy drained and my enthusiasm greatly diminished. I found myself having to mentally push myself to be positive before each group. I started feeling ineffective and increasingly depressed as a result. *Why was this happening?* I often wondered. My supervisor began noticing the change in my attitude. During one of our supervision sessions, she brought up the subject. I explained at length about my feelings of frustration and realizing that I was not making any difference by my presence. My further observation was that the patients did not seem to be interested in art therapy groups. My supervisor listened to my plight patiently and asked me what it was that I expected to get out of the groups. She further elucidated by asking me to identify if I was merely reacting to the groups' reactions to my directives and if my expectation was clearly and realistically. The question threw me, because I really had not thought about it in those terms. I was an idealistic student who wanted to save the world. When she noticed my silence and surprise, she suggested that I revisit my expectation and change it in the direction of an attainable goal, believing in my own abilities to turn the goal into reality.

Trying to be an objective and honest observer of myself—one of the benefits/curses of studying any branch of psychology—I realized that indeed I had an unrealistic expectation of the situation. In an earlier chapter, we discussed micromovements. I needed to take micromovements before I could jump. The patients' functioning levels were not in accordance with my expectations; therefore, the outcome was rather disappointing to say the least. I subconsciously set myself up for failure. What I supposed I'd see in the patients as the result of my interventions was based more on fantasy than reality. The patients did not have the capability to do what I expected, and it was admittedly unfair to demand it of them.

I decided to make a fresh start before admitting any kind of defeat. I went back with a new plan and a new attitude. My new plan involved making each session count on its own. In other words, I wanted to let the patients get the most out of the session while they were there and not expect them to recall previous directives and discussions. Within the week I was getting much higher participation from the group members and better discussions in groups. By the end of my internship, I was given the most heartfelt and the most unexpected compliment from a patient who I was convinced never heard my directives due to severe auditory hallucinations.

Once the art folders were returned back to the students, he thanked me for having offered my services and told me how helpful he had found the groups. He expressed interest in continuing art therapy in the future. There were similar sentiments from my other groups as well.

Thinking back on that experience, I still find myself fighting back tears. My goal should have been to do the best I could with the circumstances I was given, taking small steps. It was not up to me to set goals for others that were out of their reach. By changing my attitude and expectation, I was able to open up another possibility and see another solution and, as a result, feel triumphant. In other words, I set clear expectations for myself not others. I will forever be grateful to my supervisor for challenging me in my approach.

I find that whenever I apply this principle to other aspects of my life, I still get the same results. It is all about attitude and expectation, which means we have full control over our own thoughts.

> All power is from within and is therefore under our control. (Robert Collier, author of self-help and New Thought metaphysical books)

> If you don't like something change it; if you can't change it, change the way you think about it. (Mary Engelbreit, graphic artist and children's books illustrator)

One effective way of shifting your attitude and defining your goals is to state your "well-formed" desired outcomes in the positive. Do not spend time on things you do not want. Concentrate on the positive only. For example, if I want to be wealthy, I'll know that it's happened when:

> · I hear people around me talking about my lovely estate, my beautiful horses, and my Bugatti.

> · I will see to it that my bank account always exceeds $1 million.

> · I feel comfortable and relaxed at all times.

If we turn that vague want into a more specific and "well-formed" outcome (an NLP technique), then it becomes far more focused and, therefore, far more achievable.

> Change the way you look at things and the things you look at change. (Dr. Wayne Dyer, American self-help advocate, author, and lecturer)

We view the world based on our own assumptions. Even in the most basic human interactions we tend to be presumptuous. For example, if you meet someone for the first time in a gathering and feel as though her manner of greeting left a lot to be desired, you might automatically jump to the conclusion that she was a snob or did not like you, and so on and so forth.

Another way to assess this interaction would be that she may have had a lot on her mind. Perhaps she got some bad news prior to coming to the party. The point is that it's important to keep an open mind and change your mind-set. More often than not, upon future meetings, she would be friendly and down-to-earth. What you expect to see is what you will see.

When the Wright brothers came up with the idea of inventing the airplane, they did not expect it to stay on the ground. This is true of any invention. Ships are made with the expectation that they will float, not sink. Therefore, we can use this power to look at ourselves in a different way. We can think of ourselves as having the control and power over what we would like to achieve.

> All that we are is the result of what we have thought. (Buddha, spiritual teacher who founded Buddhism)

> We cannot direct the wind but we can adjust the sails. (Bertha Calloway, African-American community activist and historian)

I went to a Catholic boarding school in Malta (a small island and an old British colony on the Mediterranean Sea between Italy and Libya) for part of high school. I was the earliest "boarder" to have arrived my first day, so I had a chance to take a look around and get acquainted with the school. I was absolutely terrified and excited at the same time, because this was the first time I was living separately from my parents.

I was in the process of unpacking when the rest of the students began pouring in. Most of them already knew each other from previous years. I was the only new upper-class student. The energy and excitement of friends seeing each other was palpable, and I secretly wished I were a part of it. Finally, Sister Carla (not her real name) introduced me to the whole group once we were all in the refectory (cafeteria). It was a very embarrassing moment. It took a few weeks, but I was finally a part of the group, and by the end of the year, we were all friends. I met some amazing people there, some of whom I am still in contact with. Before we all said good-bye to each other, one of my friends admitted to having thought of me as unfriendly and somewhat of a snob. I was quite taken aback and asked her why she had thought that. The reason, she said, was that I hardly spoke to anyone and mostly kept to myself. When she realized that I could not speak English at first, she better understood my behavior, and that is when she approached me to be her friend.

We perceive what we want to perceive. Our perceptions have a direct effect on our behavior, which, in turn, are reflected in our behavior. Changing our perceptions will change the rest of the pattern.

> The only disability in life is a bad attitude. (Scott Hamilton, American figure skater and Olympic gold medalist)

> Become a possibilitarian. No matter how dark things seem to be or actually are, raise your sights and see possibilities always see them, for they're always there. (Norman Vincent Peale)

> The test of a first-rate intelligence is the ability to hold two opposed ideas in the mind at the same time, and still retain the ability to function. One should, for example, be able to see that things are hopeless and yet be determined to make them otherwise. (F. Scott Fitzgerald, American author)

Our attitudes determine our reactions and, subsequently, our emotions. We have all felt the frustration of being stuck in traffic or working in a group where we feel no one else is as committed to the project as we are. Having a sense of humor in situations that seem out of one's control can bring about the necessary change to reach the desired outcome. The following story is a great example.

"Two prime ministers are sitting in a room discussing affairs of state. Suddenly a man bursts in, apologetic with fury, shouting and stamping and banging his fist on the desk. The resident prime minister admonishes him: "Peter," he says, "kindly remember Rule Number 6," whereupon Peter is instantly restored to complete calm, apologizes, and withdraws. The politicians return to their conversation, only to be interrupted yet again twenty minutes later by an hysterical woman gesticulating wildly, her hair flying. Again the intruder is greeted with the words: "Marie, please remember Rule Number 6." Complete calm descends once more, and she too withdraws with a bow and an apology. When the scene is repeated for a third time, the visiting prime minister addresses his colleague: "My dear friend, I've seen many things in my life, but never anything as remarkable as this. Would you be willing to share with me the secret of Rule Number 6?" "Very simple," replies the resident prime minister. "Rule Number 6 is 'Don't take yourself so g—damn seriously.'" "Ah," says his visitor, "that is a fine rule." After a moment of pondering, he inquires, "And what, may I ask, are the other rules?" "There aren't any." (*The Art of Possibility,* Zander and Zander)"

I mentioned this humorous story because it is a great demonstration of both a state change and reaching the desired outcome, which, in this case, was to get the participants to calm down enough to follow the prime minister's direction. The resident prime minister brought about a catalyst for changing his staffs' attitudes and, as a result, achieved his desired outcome.

Humor can often bring about a change in attitude, as well as provide a distraction from the problem at hand, which, in turn, can be helpful in finding a solution more easily.

> I think the next best thing to solving a problem is finding some humor in it.
> (Frank A. Clark, Democratic member of the U.S. House of Representatives
> from Pensylvannia until his resignation in December 1974)

I sometimes find myself reading a humorous story, looking at a funny image, or watching a funny show as a way to recharge myself and bring myself out of creative blocks when other techniques are not as effective. This trick has always produced the desired outcome. It seems to open a channel whereby ideas begin to flow. I notice my mood improves, and my outlook changes positively.

> I like nonsense. It wakes up the brain cells. (Dr. Seuss)

The following exercise uses a technique is referred to as anchoring in NLP. I've mentioned it earlier in this book. It is a great way of bringing about a state change, which, simply put, means a change in one's attitude and state of mind.

First, get yourself into a happy state. Think of a past experiences when you were happy, construct happy thoughts and images, and visualize yourself and your loved ones smiling, laughing etc.

When you are at the peak of your state—the most intense feeling of happiness—fire off a unique anchor. For example, you could pinch your left palm. Fire off the anchor a few more times (pinch your palm a few more times) for as long as you are in that peak state.

Finally, change to a neutral state. Break your state by standing up, moving around, or shaking yourself out of it. Then repeat the process again. After numerous repetitions, the state will be anchored into you.

This process is reminiscent of the classic Pavlovian conditioning. Your anchors can be a touching a specific area, pinching, applying pressure (pushing in), saying a word, making a sound, looking at a certain image, or listening to a sound, certain music, song, etc. It can be anything that your sensory cells can pick up.

Still, a point to note is that anchors that are made of any type of physical touch are usually stronger than sounds or visual triggers, because biologically, a physical touch or pressure has a stronger sensory impact on the body.

The effectiveness of an NLP anchor that you set depends on the following:

The intensity of the state. The stronger the intensity is, the better.

Timing of the anchor. The timing of triggering the anchor is just as important. To be most effective, only trigger the anchor at its most intense moment.

Uniqueness of the anchor. Make sure your anchor is unique. It should be something that you don't normally do, see, or hear every day. For example, actions like scratching, snapping your fingers, or clapping your hands are pretty common and done quite often. Use something really unique that isn't part of your daily routine or gestures.

Number of repetitions. Naturally, the more repetitions you make, the more conditioned the anchor becomes. So make sure you do enough repetitions to make it conditioned.

Once you've mastered anchoring, you'll be able to change your state at will. In other words, you can change your attitude to the positive and once more pursue your desired outcome.

> When you want to change your circumstances, you must first change your thinking. Every time you look inside your mail expecting to see a bill, guess what—it'll be there. Each day you go out dreading the bill! You're never expecting anything great. You're thinking debt, you're expecting debt. So debt must show up so you won't think you're crazy. And every day you confirm your thought: Is debt going to be there? Yes, debt's there. Is debt going to be there? Yes, debt's there. Is debt going to be there? Yes, debt's there. Why? Because you expected debt to be there. So it showed up, because the law of attraction is always obedient to your thoughts. Do yourself a favor—expect a check! (Lisa Nichols, author, public speaker and coach)

Expectation is a powerful attractive force, because it draws things to you. Desire links you with the thing desired, and expectation pulls it into your life. Expect the things you want, not what you don't want. When you concentrate on what you do not want, you spend energy on it and, as a result, draw it to yourself.

> Whatever we expect with confidence becomes our own self-fulfilling prophecy. (Brian Tracy, self-help author)

Try the following exercise to test your attitude and expectations. You can either do this as visualization or artistically using the medium of your choice.

You are making a photo album. You are trying to organize the images to show where you've been and how far you've come. This is an accomplishment album. The first pages seem to be easy to organize. You know just where each image should go. These are the images that represent your past. The middle part is the present. Think about what images there are and where they should be. The third part of the photo album is your future. Where do you expect to be? What do you expect to be doing? How do you expect to get there? Think about what images would represent this period of time for you. If you had already reached your goal, what would the images show? Can you see what reaching your goal looks like? Can you feel what it would be like? Like the previous techniques and exercises mentioned, repetition is very helpful in forming clear images in your mind. Repetition can also help make an emotional connection between you and your mental image. Make sure your attitude is positive when engaged in this task. Positive energy will attract more positive energy. Concentrate only on what you desire.

The power of expectation works wonders. It fulfills one's intention; thus, it is most advantageous to use it in a positive way in the achievement of one's goals.

Passion

If I were to wish for anything I should not wish for wealth and power, but for the passionate seines of what can be, for the eye, whichever young and ardent, sees the possible. Pleasure disappoints, possibility never. And what wine is so sparkling, what so fragrant, what so intoxicating as possibility? (Soren Kierkegaard, Danish philosopher, theologian, and religious author interested in human psychology)

This chapter will explore the driving force necessary in every achievement and accomplishment through some well-known success stories. Passion—without passion, one will not have the drive to turn dreams into reality.

Lance Armstrong is one of the most celebrated athletes in the world. He made history in 2005 by winning the prestigious Tour de France bicycle race for the seventh consecutive year. But he is more than just an amazing cyclist with phenomenal endurance; he is also a cancer survivor who has inspired millions of people around the world.

In 1996 (*Lance Armstrong, A Biography*), Armstrong was diagnosed with cancer, and with the same fierce focus he brings to competition, he tackled his illness and won. Since then, Armstrong has become a leader in the cancer community through the Lance Armstrong Foundation, which focuses on educating the public about early cancer detection and raising money to find a cure for the disease that kills more than half a million people in the United States each year.

Armstrong's mother bought him his first bike when he was seven years old. He immediately began to ride it every day and soon proved that he was a natural athlete.

Barely in his teens, Armstrong was already competing in amateur cycling races. He also participated in other sports and entered triathlon competitions. However, Armstrong's real love was biking. He began training with more-experienced riders and quickly rose in the amateur ranks of cycling. Armstrong drew so much attention that when he was a senior at Plano East High School, he was approached by the US Olympic development team and invited to train in Colorado Springs, Colorado.

Armstrong did not remain an amateur for long. In 1992, when he turned professional, Armstrong was asked to join the Motorola cycling team, and in July 1993, the young cyclist made his debut at the race that would make him a future celebrity—the Tour de France.

The Tour de France is a three-week, 2,287-mile race that takes place in twenty stages, with competitors winding through the French countryside and pedaling up and down steep mountain landscapes. It is considered to be the most prestigious cycling event in the world and is a grueling physical challenge.

Although he did not finish the race, Armstrong did win one of the stages, making him the third-youngest participant ever to do so.

On October 2, 1996, just weeks after his twenty-fifth birthday, Armstrong was diagnosed with testicular cancer that had also spread to his lungs, abdomen, lymph nodes, and brain. Doctors predicted a slim chance for recovery—less than 40 percent. Armstrong, however, was not ready to give up. He read everything he could about the disease and changed his diet, giving up coffee, dairy products, and red meat. After consulting his doctors, Armstrong decided to forego the traditional treatment for brain tumors, which is radiation. Side effects from radiation can include a loss of balance and a scarring of the lungs, which would mean that he would probably never race again. Instead, doctors performed surgery to remove the tumors and then administered an alternative and aggressive form of chemotherapy.

Between rounds of chemotherapy, Armstrong continued to ride his bicycle as much as he could, and he never lost his determination to return to professional racing. At the same time, he was on an emotional roller coaster. As he told *Time* in 1999, "I had the same emotions when I was sick as I have as a competitive athlete. At first I was angry, then I felt motivated and driven to get better. And then when I knew I was getting better, I knew I was winning." Armstrong's determination to win paid off when, in February 1997, he was declared cancer-free.

Getting back into training, Armstrong pushed himself harder than ever, and he went on to conquer the Tour de France seven consecutive times. He has been the only athlete to have done so.

This story, as mentioned at the beginning of this chapter, seemed very compelling, because it demonstrates not only the power of perseverance, attitude, and a clear vision, but also passion. Passion is an essential part on the road to realizing your dream. It is the vital force, the greatest desire that propels us to go forth and take action. It is the fuel that runs the engine of our paths. It is the necessary ingredient in achieving one's highest potential.

> Chase down your passion like it's the last bus of the night. (Glade Byron Addams, poet)

> If there is no passion in your life, then have you really lived? Find your passion, whatever it may be. Become it, and let it become you and you will find great things happen FOR you, TO you and BECAUSE of you. (T. Alan Armstrong)

Many of you may be familiar with the name Paulo Coelho, the best-selling author of *The Alchemist*. As a teenager, he wanted to be a writer. Upon telling his parents, he was met with opposition. His parents wished him to pursue engineering or law; however, Paulo had no interest in those fields. He had always dreamed about being a writer. His introversion and opposition to following a traditional path led to his parents to commit him to a mental institution at age seventeen. He managed to escape three times before his release at age twenty.

Coelho did enroll in law school at his parents' wish, but he was very unhappy and dropped out of the program.

In 1986, Coelho walked the five hundred-plus-mile Road of Santiago de Compostela in northwestern Spain, which was a turning point in his life. On the path, Coelho had a kind of spiritual awakening. One year after this experience, he wrote *The Alchemist*. *The Alchemist* has gone on to sell more than 30 million copies, becoming one of the best-selling books in history. It has been translated into more than sixty-seven languages, winning the Guinness World Record for most-translated book by a living author.

"My dream was, and still is, to be a writer," Coelho said in an interview.

When you follow your dream, give it your all. Be passionate. That enthusiasm alone can lift your spirit and mind into new possibilities. It is the perfect catalyst for attitude change. The expectations change, and so do the feelings. One cannot help but feel uplifted, and the road suddenly seems to be a lot smoother.

> Follow your passion, and success will follow you. (Arthur Buddhold, author)

> The more intensely we feel about an idea or a goal, the more assuredly the idea, buried deep in our subconscious, will direct us along the path to its fulfillment. (Earl Nightingale, American motivational speaker and author)

All around us is energy. The universe is vibrant with creative power. But how do we tap into this source? Where can we find a power outlet for liveliness? Do we have to pump up the energy ourselves and carry it around with us, or can we catch the current of some other source outside of ourselves?

Let's suppose for a moment that expressive energy flows everywhere, that it is the only way for the continuation of life, and that any kind of block or resistance to be a part of it comes from within us. However, if we want to be true participants in this source, we must take these two steps: First, we must pinpoint where we are holding back and let go. Release all the limitations and barriers of self that keep us separate and let the vital energy of passion course through us, connecting us to the universe. Second, we must participate wholly and completely, allowing ourselves to be the portal, the channel to influence and shape the flow of passion into a new expression for the world.

When we live with passion, following our dreams and pushing away limitations, we are full participants in the world. We beckon to us what we want the most by opening up to the possibilities, keeping a clear vision, and believing wholeheartedly that it is within our grasp.

> Don't ask yourself what the world needs; ask yourself what makes you come alive. And then go and do that. Because what the world needs is people who have come alive. (Harold Whitman, philosopher)

Emotion is pure energy and power, and when combined with visualization, it makes things happen a lot faster. Once you're aware of this principle as seen in your own experience, you'll feel empowered, and your confidence in your own ability to effectively change the course of your life increases. As a result, you'll be able to purse your dreams with more conviction. Therefore, remember you now can purse your dreams with greater enthusiasm, because you know that the first step is to actually have them. So, go ahead and dream.

A Personal Story

Ever since I can recall, I have had a love of writing, or perhaps I should clarify it as creating. I, like other children, had a very active imagination and spent many quality moments inside my fantastic adventures. I remember making up stories about the tree trunk that was bent over the fence between our yard and the neighbor's. I pretended that it was a horse, my horse. We'd go places together and encounter many adventures. My horse even had a name—Samson.

My Barbie also had a rather avant-garde wardrobe, because I was the sole designer. Being younger than nine years of age at the time did not lend much room to professional craftsmanship. The furniture in her house (a big cardboard box) followed the same principle. I would spend countless hours immersed in perfect bliss making those designs—anything from furniture to lamps and carpets. I can still clearly remember that feeling as though it happened yesterday.

Adolescence offered a rather different menu, so the appetizers were put aside. Unfortunately, the main dish was never served. There was much change and turmoil, not necessarily in the sense of teenage angst but life-altering changes, such as being uprooted several times. I did take refuge in music (piano), although none of my own composition. Still, the therapeutic and balancing effect was undeniable.

My family moved during the early part of my adolescence, which made it difficult for me to feel established and rooted. It is important for a teenager to be part of a group and find validation for her reality and beliefs. I consider myself rather sociable and enjoy the company of others most of the time, but this continued period of transition and change made it difficult to form lasting bonds of friendship. Writing was forgotten, not even as an escape. Creativity of any other kind was put on a shelf somewhere in the basement of my mind behind a closed door.

At long last, my family decided on a place to stay, and roots began to sprout. College—the perfect venue to design one's future prospects—came into the picture. But this wasn't true in my case, initially at least. I was raised with the mind-set that I should consider studying something practical, because that would give me a better possibility of employment and financial independence. I studied sciences at first, contemplating a future in medicine. I always enjoyed biology and achieved high marks; however, I soon discovered that it was not the path for me. My other interest was psychology and human behavior; it also had a stronger pull, so I declared it my major.

After graduation, I began working with a group of family therapists. It brought me in contact with such fascinating people and ideas, as well as my first encounter with NLP. I also got married. My husband is an artist. After years of keeping that basement door closed, I began remembering that I had put something there on the shelf. His creative energy brought that back to my consciousness.

Graduate school was always an ambition. Going through a college catalog one day I discovered art therapy. I must admit that I had been ignorant about expressive therapies programs up to that point, but the idea seemed ideal. It combined two things I loved, so I applied. The main requirement for graduation was submitting a thesis paper (referred to as a practicum paper in my program), as is the case with most graduate programs. I was at once excited and mortified by the idea. I finally had a chance to write, albeit within the constraints of the APA format. But all the while, I wondered whether my writing skills were good enough. The program itself was heavily based on writing, which I had difficulty with due to insufficient elaboration. I was constantly reminded that I needed to further explain and expand on my analyses of the topics presented. This feeling of inadequacy remained my constant companion.

My experience in writing proved to be less than satisfactory when I had to do my thesis project. My paper had to be resubmitted with an entirely new theme due to a major mistake on my part. My months of planning and collecting artwork were discarded. I became terrified of writing and lost confidence in my abilities altogether, but my graduation depended on writing the thesis. Therefore, my fear was reluctantly put on the shelf until I could attend to it.

Thinking back to my thesis paper, I can now confess that deep down I expected to be unsuccessful. I was convinced that I was not a good writer, and the paper would never be good enough. I remember clearly seeing in my mind's eye that there was going to be a problem with the paper, and my work was going to be rejected. I was not consciously aware that I was not passionate about my subject matter, which made it more difficult to write the paper in the first paper. I did not believe that my subject was interesting enough, because I had not really thought about it on my own. It felt more like a chore, something to be done so I could begin my professional life; as a result, I received my outcome accordingly. I only concentrated on what I did not want rather than the reverse.

Several years passed, during which my compositions were reduced to writing progress reports and diagnostic plans. I did very little in terms of creativity, and in a way, I fell into a pattern. I shall refer to this pattern as my comfort zone. It was much easier to follow a kind of guideline, a formula if you will, than having to think creatively, especially since I no longer felt confident about my talents. Designing directives and doing artwork in groups did not feel creative to me. Somewhere along the way I lost sight of my passion. I fell into a routine. This state came to an abrupt stop, however, when I was laid off from work.

Now, several years have gone by again and I am currently self-employed. I am involved in the creative process on a daily basis and cannot believe I ever functioned without it. As for my writing, a few months ago I attended a webinar (seminar or workshop offered over the Internet) about writing, which I found very helpful and encouraging. The main principle emphasized that it must be important to the writer and done for the writer by the writer. In other words, I must do it for myself, because I love it. This is, for me, first and foremost. It is my dream. That was the key.

The group participating in the webinar also got a chance to collaborate on a project. The result was a book released in time for Christmas 2010, which instantly made it to the top of the Amazon Bestseller list (*The Gratitude Book Project*). What better validation can there be?

I have a blog now (www.mydanglingparticiple.com), which has proven to be a great venue for my creativity. Every time I write a new post I feel my spirit so uplifted that it carries me through the whole day. I've opened the door to that basement room in my mind and yanked my creativity off that shelf. I am finally doing what I truly love and cannot fathom ever abandoning it. This book is also a testament to that.

> Renew your passions daily. (Teri Guillemets U.S. quotation anthologist, creator of The Quote Garden)

> Every great dream begins with a dreamer. Always remember, you have within you the strength, the patience, and the passion to reach for the stars to change the world. (Harriet Tubman, African-American abolitionist, humanitarian and union spy during THe American Civil War)

The life force for humankind is the passionate energy to connect, express, and communicate. Full participation is that energy at work. Let that energy course through you and lift you to the highest level of your creativity to follow your dreams.

Try the following exercise to tap into your passionate energy:

Take a piece of paper. Any size will do, but 8½" x 11" is preferable. You can use any type of color—for example, colored pencil, cray pas, pastels, or paint —it is up to you.

Make sure there are no distractions around you.

Now, think for a moment about what you're passionate about. If you were to represent it with a color, what would it be? Would it be just one color or multiple colors? Are they blended? Does it have a particular shape? Put them all on the paper. Don't be concerned about how your work looks. When you are thinking of your subject, how do you feel? Look at your finished work. Does it represent your internal feeling? If so, you might wish to put it somewhere so you can see it every day. If not, make sure that it does. Let this be a daily reminder of how you can feel when you do what you love.

Watching

The title of this chapter could also be called meditation. This may seem like an oxymoron, but the two are rather similar. While meditation is an act of contemplation, continuous thought, and musing, watching is active observation with focused attention. It encourages a meditative state. If you watch something intently, you will be transported to another state.

> No great work has ever been produced except after a long interval of still and musing meditation. (Walter Bagehot, English businessman, essayist and journalist)

Meditation is like watching your thoughts. It's centering, focusing, and channeling your thoughts either through silence or chanting. It is a way of relaxation, as well as concentration—letting the inspirational energy go through you so you can be connected to the creative force.

Meditation can also be used in a therapeutic manner. We have all heard stories about healing though mediation and concentration—healing through thought. It is not that uncommon. We've already discussed the power of imagination, which is the power of thought. Did we not attest to it having a strong bearing on changing our state and attitude? Seeing in your mind's eye what you want the end result to be? Then it should not come as a shock that thought can heal.

> The question frequently asked is, "When a person has manifested a disease in the body temple or some kind of discomfort in their life, can it be turned around through the power of 'right' thinking?" And the answer is absolutely, yes. (Michael Bernard Beckwith, African-American New Thought minister)

It is not to say that the field of medicine is ineffective and should be dismissed. Healing through the mind can work compatibly with medicine. It is important to point this out.

Medicine is crucial in many circumstances. If pain is involved, then medicine can be helpful in removing that pain so attention can be turned to becoming healthy. This goes back to the idea of concentrating on what one wants. In this case, it would be health. Thinking perfect health is something anybody can do inwardly, regardless of what is happening around her.

> We could say that meditation doesn't have a reason or doesn't have a purpose. In this respect it's unlike almost all other things we do except perhaps making music and dancing. When we make music we don't do it in order to reach a certain point, such as the end of the composition. If that were the purpose of music then obviously the fastest players would be the best. Also, when we are dancing we are not aiming to arrive at a particular place on the floor as in a journey. When we dance, the journey itself is the point, as when we play music the playing itself is the point. And exactly the same thing is true in meditation. Meditation is the discovery that the point of life is always arrived at in the immediate moment. (Alan Watts, American writer, thinker, and interpreter of Zen Buddhism)

We have come to understand the principle of meditation; however, the application or the practice may be more difficult to master at first. How do we narrow down our thoughts to one or two? We are bombarded daily with information from numerous sources, be it the Internet, radio, television, or newspapers; the list is endless.

Here is a simple exercise that can help you focus your thoughts:

Take a blank notepad.

Write any three sentences on a blank page. You'll notice that you can easily read what you have written.

Now write another ten sentences on the same page. Then cross out a few sentences and write them again. Then cross out another few sentences. Continue to do this until your page is so crowded that you can hardly read or make sense of anything written there.

Now focus on the page and try to pick out the fist sentences you had written.

The blank page represents your mind, which can get overcrowded with thoughts and information very quickly, hence the crossing out and adding new sentences. Once you can concentrate on just a few or even one sentence, you will have been able to push the others out. Even as you engage in going through these steps, you will be tuning out other distractions.

Once you feel comfortable with this exercise, try it mentally. The blank page is your mind, and the writings are your thoughts. Try to single specific thoughts out and concentrate on them. With repetition, you will soon be able to tap into that quiet place in your mind with only a thought or two.

> Practice meditation regularly. Meditation leads to eternal bliss. Therefore meditate, meditate. (Swami Sivananda, Hindu spiritual teacher)

You can now imagine the possibility of concentrating on your goal using meditation.

A similar meditative state can be achieved through watching. By watching, I am referring to looking at a particular thing or things, such as a stream or the clouds, with no judgment. Be with that thing in the moment and let it be, having no particular purpose at the time but to be in the moment of whatever comes to your senses and being aware of it.

You can also be the watcher of your thoughts and emotions. While the thoughts are in your head, the emotions have a strong physical component and are primarily felt in the body. Ask yourself, *What is going on inside me?* Notice your emotions. Allow them to be there and be aware of them but not controlled by them. Become the observer of their presence. Be present in the now, in the moment.

In order to create a meditative state, you must be relaxed. Relaxation is crucial in meditation. The following exercise is a great way to induce deep relaxation and can be used as a practice for its own purpose. Repetition will be very useful in bringing about this feeling of tranquility and calm.

Give yourself about five to ten minutes during the day when you can be somewhere quiet. Sit with your back well supported and loosen any tight clothing. Let your arms rest on your lap. You can also lie on the floor if that is more comfortable. Loosen any tight clothing.

Take a deep breath and let your shoulders relax. Become aware of it. Now take another deep breath and feel your facial muscles relax from your forehead to your chin. Breathe slowly and easily.

If ideas or feelings come to your head, act as though they are a sound from a distance. Acknowledge their presence, but you do not need attend to them at the moment.

Notice your breathing as it enters your nostrils (you can focus on each breath separately), and then notice it when you breathe out. Repeat this until you have done at least four cycles (inhale and exhale). With each cycle, focus on different areas of your body, such as your neck, limbs, buttocks, and all the way down to your feet.

Now let your breathing return to normal and enjoy the relaxed state you have created.

Once this relaxation exercise becomes a natural routine for you, you can simply feel relaxed so that you can contemplate on your thoughts next time. Simply listen to your thoughts and allow your inspirations to flow into your awareness. Let any idea, however silly, come to your mind. Think about what inspires you and makes you feel excited and passionate. What are your aspirations? What kinds of activities stimulate your creativity? Choose a method, any method—like drawing, writing, taking pictures, etc.—and then let your intuition lead the way. You will be surprised at the wisdom in your own internal guidance. Trust this process.

It's About the Process

We have all experienced the creative and the personally enriching potential of art at one point or another. As a child, you probably enjoyed making collages out of cut up paper or drawing with crayons. As an adult, you may not consider yourself to be creative as an artist, but you most likely have experienced some therapeutic aspects of it in your daily life. Perhaps you sketch, take photographs, or doodle in the corner of your notebook and have realized that it soothes and relaxes you. All of these are methods of self-expression that change your state of being and tap your intuitive and creative powers.

When one is engaged in making art, whatever the medium may be, one is transported into another level of consciousness. The mind is open and receptive, and the spirit is in a heightened state. It is not so much about the outcome as it is about the journey and the action of creating. This state is referred to in art therapy as the process. The approach subscribing to this school of thought is known as art as therapy. It is believed that the process of creating is in itself a therapeutic state. Anyone who has ever made an attempt at producing a painting will have realized that just mixing the colors and putting shapes on the canvas has a restorative power.

The same can be said when following a goal and trying to reach a particular destination. It is also useful, sometimes necessary, to be mindful of the steps and the path one is taking. It is not just the outcome that is important, but the way one has gotten there. There are many valuable lessons to be learned on the way to one's goal. The expression "stop and smell the roses" is the perfect articulation of this fact.

Art therapists observe their clients' participation in groups or individual sessions, all the while being watchful of how the clients approach the materials, what they do with them, how they interact with other group members, and the outcome of the given directive. In other words, they pay particular attention to the process of making art. In fact, it is as important to see (go through) the process as it is to produce an outcome.

As in the case of art therapy, the lessons we learn and the things we observe and experience along the journey—the process—are what help us reach our ultimate goals. These observations are essential in our paths. The next time you are engaged in something creative, let yourself go through that process and try to be mindful of it—a fact that was also mentioned in the previous chapter.

What makes the choice of being in the moment difficult is that you must forgo your need to know. The ego gives you a false sense of knowing, which is comforting, even though the ego does not really know where life is going or what will happen next. So, all you really have to surrender is the pretense of knowing, not actually knowing. The fact is that no one knows what the next moment holds; that's the challenge of being in the "now," as well as its joy. To be in the moment, you have to be willing to just be and react naturally to what comes out of your flow without pretending to know what to do next or what would happen. The fact is that you've never known what would happen. Admitting this will allow you to move out of your ego-centered mind and into the moment where you can feel peaceful and connected to the surrounding energy.

We shall refer to this process as allowing. The reason is that one must allow oneself to experience—allow projects to take the time they should, allow your own process to bring new discovery, allow the darker moments to lead you toward the light, allow your fears to pass and your strengths to grow, and finally, allow yourself to be in the moment.

The following exercise is a great way to get you started in noticing your own process.

In an earlier chapter we visited mandalas. We shall use one for this segment, too. Take a piece of paper, any size will do. Draw a circle using a plate or a string attached to your pencil. Once you've outlined it, you can begin your work. Choose any medium you prefer, such as colored pencil, crayon, pens, paint, etc. Contemplate your circle for a few minutes. You can work inside the circle, outside, or both. You can even turn the circle into something. The main objective is to pay attention to what you're doing while you are doing it. Notice the way you are engaged in this task and the feelings that arise during this period—in other words, the process. Once you are done, assess both your outcome and your feelings. It is this feeling that was the objective. It is the art as therapy approach that is used to offer the therapeutic benefits of creativity.

The expression "stop and smell the roses" refers to this matter. Along the journey to our goals, we must sometimes pay attention to the signs and dirt roads connecting to our track and other things we pass along the path. Noticing them can be as important as our destination itself.

Course of Actions Revisited

In response to those who say to stop dreaming and face reality, I say keep dreaming and make reality. (Kristian Kan, author)

Days go by and turn into weeks; weeks turn into months, and months turn into years. Seasons come and go. This is time passing by. It is always moving forward. It waits for no one. It's unforgiving.

How many times have you dreamed about that one thing you would love to do if only you had the time? Time—did we not establish that it does not wait for anyone? It's like a carriage being pulled by an invisible force that makes no stops. You must jump on and hold on tight. The only comfort is that it does not discriminate. It cares very little whether you are young or old, rich or poor.

Ride into your life on a creative cycle full of juice, abundance and ecstatic wonderment. (SARK- *Living Juicy*)

No dream is foolish. The only foolish thing is not following it. One must be confident and believe wholeheartedly that it is attainable.

The best angle from which to approach any problem is the try-angle. (author unknown, www.quotegarden.com)

A thousand words will never make as big and lasting an impression as one action. Couple your intentions with action. If you don't do it, you don't really believe it. Some people spend all of their time searching for what is right but can't seem to find the time to practice it. Always be mindful of the fact that your life story is written with your actions not with a pen. To do nothing is to be nothing.

Action overcomes fear.

When we challenge our fears, we master them. When we wrestle with our problems, they lose their grip on us. When we dare to confront the things that scare us, we open the door to personal liberty. (Anonymous)

Learning to identify procrastination, fear, and resistance is important in helping you to move forward. Procrastination is a learned behavior. You pick up and learn all sorts of habits from childhood. If you are conscious of it and accept it, then you can take the first step and move forward. This happens alongside of being confident and believing in what you want to achieve.

It is one thing to have an idea, but it's quite another to trust your idea and follow where it leads. Following your passion means taking risks. Whether you take impulsive or calculated risks, there is an element of fear, because the risk could turn out to be positive or negative. However, the important fact to bear in mind is to be confident in your ability to turn your dream into reality. Letting fear take over will render you mentally paralyzed and thus unable to take the next step.

To be a positive risk taker, you must practice, honor your successes, and learn and grow from your mistakes and mishaps. You must learn to trust yourself so you can persist. Passion has great power to keep us committed. Follow your dream, take the necessary risks, and you will progress.

A Useful Ritual/Practice

Do you notice how limited thinking and fear of being wrong or looking foolish hinder your creative goals? What beliefs help or keep you from taking risks, trying something different, changing direction, or following your own course? Start by collecting examples of times when you have been particularly persistent and successful. What were the skills or beliefs that helped you to stay committed to your goal in the face of obstacles? Identify these strengths and post them in a place when you can see them on a regular basis.

You have brains in your head.

You have feet in your shoes.

You can steer yourself in any direction you choose.

You're on your own.

And you know what you know.

You are the guy who'll decide where to go. (Dr. Seuss)

Believing in your abilities and knowing that you can reach your goal is essential to getting there. You must first identify the fears and then set them free. Fears only hold you back. Letting go of everything that holds you back opens you up to possibilities and brings out your talents.

We all have talent in some way. Creativity is built into every one of us; it's part of our design. When you choose not to use the creative powers you have, you live less of the life intended for you. Investing in your talent and beliefs is investing in yourself. This is a positive step. Spending positive energy on yourself will attract more positive toward you, according to the Law of Attraction.

Taking the first step—that beginning moment—is the only hurdle we need to overcome. Sometimes it takes several beginnings before it develops its own momentum. No matter how many times you find yourself beginning, the important point to remember is to allow yourself that chance. Do not let fear stop you. There are no correct beginnings, only your beginnings. Believe in the fact that you will succeed in finding your own way, and you shall.

> When you are describing, A shape, or sound, or tint; Don't state the matter plainly, But put it in a hint; And learn to look at all

> things, With a sort of mental squint. (Lewis Carroll, English author, mathematician, logician, Anglican deacon, and photographer)

> It's so hard when I have to, and so easy when I want to. (Annie Gottlier, author)

With the right attitude and the expectation that your desired outcome is attainable, the path seems to get easier. When you keep your mind open to the possibility, you can begin to find new ways of accomplishing your goal. In most cases, the attitude is the main difference between success and failure. If you've ever worked with a group of people who share a similar goal, you will see how effective the right attitude is. The group belief in its success can open up new possibilities and solutions.

> Attitudes are contagious. Are yours worth catching? (Dennis and Wendy Mannering, authors)

Just as a positive attitude can influence others to move forward, a negative attitude can have the reverse effect. One must stay true to her convictions and believe in the possibilities.

He who has so little knowledge of human nature as to seek happiness by changing anything but his own disposition will waste his life in fruitless efforts. (Samuel Johnson, British author, poet, essayist, and moralist)

It is all about how you see your situation. If you cannot change what you see, you need to change how you see it; change the attitude.

Without passion man is a mere latent force and possibility, like the flint which awaits the shock of the iron before it can give forth its spark. (Amiel, Swiss philosopher, poet, and critic)

Have you noticed how much easier and more pleasant any task seems when you are enthusiastic about it? You no longer have to force yourself to do it. You gladly do it, because you enjoy it. Does following your ultimate goal deserve any less? Be passionate about what you do. Give it all you have. Feel the flow of energy go through you and feel the excitement in your veins. With passion and enthusiasm, any task will seem easier, and the path will feel a little less difficult.

Meditate to keep your mind focused and let possibilities come your way. Any activity that may have that meditative quality can be beneficial—perhaps a creative project or listening to music. Feel the readiness and receptivity of your state of mind and embrace it.

The world needs dreamers and the world needs doers. But above all, the world needs dreamers who do. (Sarah Ban Breathnach, *Simple Abundance: A Daybook of Comfort and Joy*, 1996)

When you truly believe in your dreams, you will find a way to overcome your fears and resistances and find possibilities to reach your goal. It may take longer than you estimated or be more difficult that you expected, but your attitude and enthusiasm will keep you focused and motivated to keep moving forward.

Surrendering to life isn't hard at all. It happens simply and naturally whenever we stop paying attention to the mind's version of life, itself, as it is coming out of the Now. There is something else to do besides Think! And that is to notice, to be aware of what is happening now. Notice, look, feel, listen, sense, and give yourself fully to the experience you are having, and you will drop into the Now. (Gina Lake, author, spiritual teacher)

It is about the process. It is about what happens while you are trying to achieve your goal. Be aware of it. In other words, take notice what you are experiencing.

I try to learn from the past, but I plan for the future by focusing exclusively on the present. That's where the fun is. (Donald Trump, American businessman and television personality)

Remember then: there is only one time that is Important—Now! It is the most important time because it is the only time when we have any power. (Leo Tolstoy, Russian writer)

Remember that most learning takes place while you are trying to reach your goal. Pay attention to it, feel it, and let yourself be in it.

References

Barber, Vicki, *Explore Yourself Through Art: Creative Projects to Help You Achieve Personal Insight & Growth & Promote Problem Solving*, Carroll & Brown Limited, 2002.

Bradbury, Andrew, *Develop Your NLP Skills*, Kogan Page, 2006.

Buchalter, Susan I., *A Practical Art Therapy*, Jessica Kingsley Publishers, 2004.

Byrne, Rhonda, *The Secret*, Beyond Words Publishing, 2006.

Dooley, Mike, *Infinite Possibilities: The Art of Living Your Dreams*, Atria Books, 2009.

Fincher, Susanne F., *Coloring Mandalas 1*, Shambhala, 2000.

Gutman, Bill, *Lance Armstrong: A Biography*, Simon Pulse, 2009.

Lake, Gina, *What About Now? Reminders for Being in the Moment*, Endless Satsang Foundation, 2009.

Gunning, Stephanie, *Audacious Creativity: 50 Ways to Liberate Your Soulful Creative Energy and How It Can Transform Your Life*, Creative Blast Press, NY, 2008.

Mason, John, *Believe You Can, The Power of Positive Attitude*, Spire, 2010.

McMeekin, Gail, *The 12 Secrets of Highly Creative Women*, Conari Press, 2000.

Malchiodi, Cathy A., ATR, L.P.C.C., *The Art Therapy Sourcebook*, The McGraw-Hill Companies, 2007.

SARK, *Living Juicy, Daily Morsels for Your Creative Soul,* Celestial Arts, Berkley, CA 1994.

Zander, Rosamund Stone, Zander, Benjamin, *The Art of Possibility,* Penguin Books, 2000.

Other references were collections found from different quotation sites on the Internet such as http://www.thinkexist.com and http://*www.brainyquote.com.*

Maryam's blog: www.mydanglingparticiple.com